Wrestling

Joanne Mattern

Rourke
Publishing LLC
Vero Beach, Florida 32964

www.rourkepublishing.com

PHOTO CREDITS: © Bruce Livingstone: Title Page; © Brandon Laufenberg: Header; © Timothy R. Nichols: page 4 top; © Razberry: page 4 bottom; © Nancy K. Lane-Feldner/www.splitsecondsports.com: page 5, 8, 9, 11, 13 top, 14, 15, 19; © Max Blain: page 7; © Charles T. Bennett: page 10; © Danielle Hobeika: page 6, 12, 13 bottom, 16, 17, 18; © Brandon Laufenberg: page 16 top, 17 top; © Christine Balderas: page 20 bottom; © Lurii Konoval: page 21; Courtesy: U.S. Air Force photo/Rob Bussard: page 22 top; Courtesy U.S. Army/Tim Hipps: page 22 bottom

Edited by Kelli Hicks

Cover design by Nicola Stratford: bdpublishing.com
Interior design by Renee Brady

Library of Congress Cataloging-in-Publication Data

Mattern, Joanne, 1963-
  Wrestling / Joanne Mattern.
    p. cm. -- (Action sports)
  ISBN 978-1-60472-399-1
  1. Wrestling--Juvenile literature. I. Title.
  GV1195.3.M325 2009
  796.812--dc22

                          2008016357

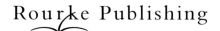

Rourke Publishing

www.rourkepublishing.com – rourke@rourkepublishing.com
Post Office Box 3328. Vero Beach. FL 32964

Table of Contents

An Ancient Sport

Wrestling is one of the oldest sports in the world. Wrestlers use their muscles to push each other down. The goal is to pin, or hold, the other wrestler to the mat.

People have been wrestling for at least 15,000 years. The ancient Greeks enjoyed wrestling. Wrestling was one of the sports in the first

Olympics. The Olympics started in ancient Greece thousands of years ago.

Thousands of years ago, the ancient Romans came to Greece. They learned about wrestling. Later, wrestling spread all over Europe.

Did You Know...

When people in Europe moved to North America, wrestling came too.

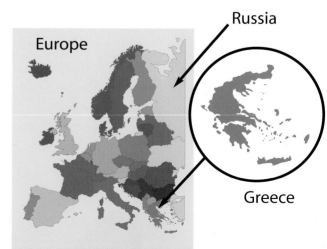

Russia

Europe

Greece

Wrestling clubs allow kids to start wrestling when they are five years old.

Different Types of Wrestling

There are three ways to wrestle. These three types are **Greco-Roman**, **freestyle**, and **folkstyle**.

Greco-Roman wrestling is the oldest kind of wrestling. This kind of wrestling was popular in ancient Greece and ancient Rome. In Greco-Roman wrestling, the wrestlers cannot use their legs to pin an **opponent**. They have to push each other down only using their arms.

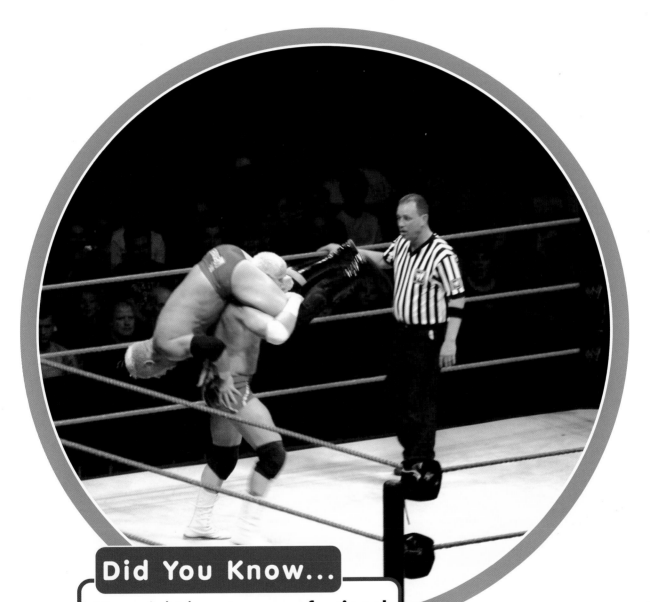

Did You Know...

You might have seen **professional** wrestling on TV. This is not the same sport as **amateur** wrestling. You will learn about amateur wrestling in this book.

Freestyle wrestling has fewer rules than Greco-Roman wrestling. In this type of wrestling, wrestlers can use both their arms and their legs.

Folkstyle wrestling also lets wrestlers use their legs and arms. This kind of wrestling is a lot like freestyle wrestling. But some of the rules are different. Folkstyle is the most popular kind of wrestling in the United States. This is the type of wrestling usually done in high schools and colleges.

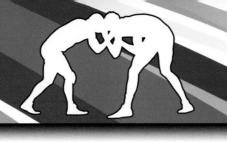

Did You Know...

The first wrestling **competition** in the United States was held in 1888.

Clothes and Equipment

You do not need a lot of equipment to wrestle. The **uniform** is very simple. Most wrestlers wear a **singlet**. A singlet is a tight-fitting, one-piece outfit. Some wrestlers also wear knee pads. Folkstyle wrestlers have to wear **head gear**. Knee pads and head gear protect wrestlers from getting hurt. Wrestlers also wear special shoes. Wrestling shoes grip the mat. They help the wrestler keep his or her balance.

head gear

singlet

shoes

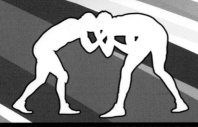

Did You Know...

It is against the rules for a wrestler to grab an opponent's singlet.

Wrestling **matches** take place on a round mat. The mat is made of thick foam. It has two circles. The inside circle is small. That is  where wrestlers stand at the start of a match. Once the match starts, wrestlers can move around the whole mat. If a wrestler steps off the mat, he or she is **out of bounds**.

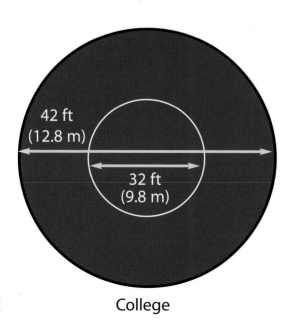

42 ft
(12.8 m)

32 ft
(9.8 m)

College

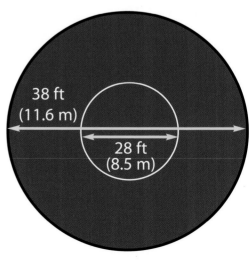

38 ft
(11.6 m)

28 ft
(8.5 m)

High school

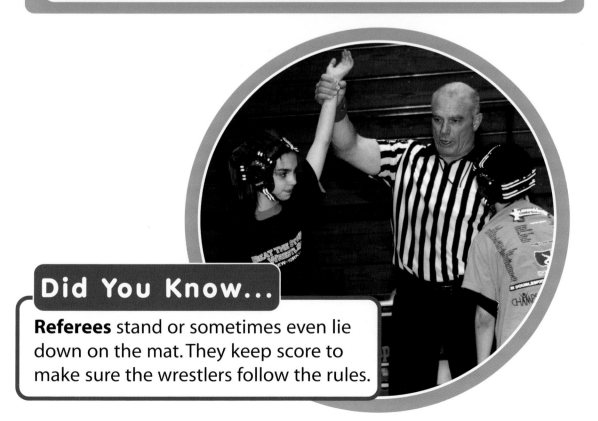

Did You Know...

Referees stand or sometimes even lie down on the mat. They keep score to make sure the wrestlers follow the rules.

Matches

Wrestling matches usually do not last very long. A Greco-Roman or freestyle match usually has two **periods**. Each period lasts three minutes. Folkstyle matches usually have three periods. Each period lasts two minutes. Matches with younger wrestlers might have periods that only last a minute.

Scoring a Match

Takedown (pushing your opponent to the mat): 2 points

Near Fall (almost pinning your opponent): 2-3 points

Escape (getting away from your opponent): 1 point

Reversal (getting away from being pinned and taking control of your opponent): 2 points

Penalties (when you or your opponent breaks a rule): 1-2 points

Attack and Defend

A wrestler wants to get **control** over his or her opponent. He or she tries to hold the opponent. A hold is when you grasp the opponent with your hands, arms, or legs. Your opponent cannot move. A throw is when you force your opponent down to the mat. Then you try to pin your opponent. You want to hold his or her shoulders down on the mat for two seconds. If you do, you win the match!

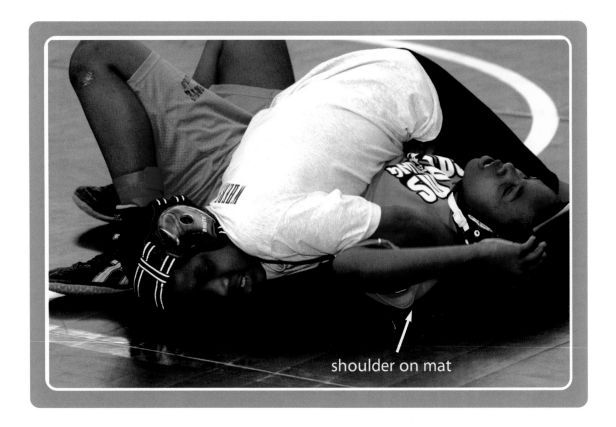

shoulder on mat

Wrestlers also defend against each other. Wrestlers try to twist out of a hold. They can push back against their opponent. If a wrestler can keep his or her balance and twist away, he or she will not get pinned.

Wrestling Competitions

Many high schools and colleges have wrestling teams. During a competition, each wrestler on the team has his or her match. At the end of the competition, officials add up the players' scores. The team with the most points wins.

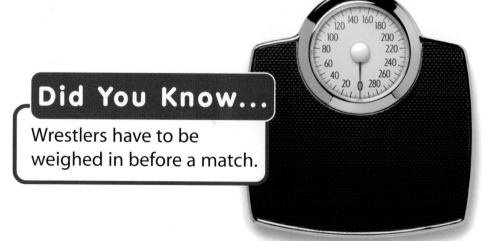

Did You Know...

Wrestlers have to be weighed in before a match.

Players in a competition are ranked in different classes. A class includes wrestlers of the same weight or age. It would not be fair to have a heavy wrestler compete against a small wrestler, or an older wrestler compete against a younger one!

The Olympics

Wrestling is a popular sport at the summer **Olympics**. The ancient Greeks wrestled in the ancient Olympics. When the **modern** Olympics started in 1904, wrestling was one of the sports. It still is an Olympic sport today. There are two styles of wrestling in the Olympics. One is Greco-Roman wrestling. The other is freestyle wrestling.

Did You Know...

Only men wrestled in the Olympics until 2004. That year, the Olympics added women's wrestling.

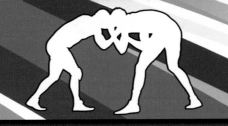

Glossary

amateur (AM-uh-chur): not paid

competition (kom-puh-TIH-shuhn): a contest

control (kuhn-TROLE): to make someone do what you want

folkstyle (FOKE-stile): a type of wrestling popular in the United States

freestyle (FREE-stile): a type of wrestling in which wrestlers can use their legs to hold an opponent

Greco-Roman (GRECK-oh ROH-muhn): a type of wrestling in which wrestlers may not use their legs to hold an opponent

head gear (HED GEER): protective equipment that covers the head

matches (MACH-uz): games or sporting competitions

neutral position (NOO-truhl puh-ZIH-shuhn): the position wrestlers take at the start of a match

Olympics (uh-LIM-piks): competitions held every two years for athletes from all over the world

opponent (uh-POH-nuhnt): a person who is against you in a fight

out of bounds (OWT UV BOWNDZ): outside the playing field or area

penalties (PEN-uhl-teez): punishments

periods (PIHR-ee-uhdz): short parts of a sports competition

professional (pruh-FESH-uh-nuhl): paid to take part in a sport

referees (ref-uh-REEZ): people who supervise a sports match or game

singlet (SING-let): a tight, one-piece outfit worn by wrestlers

stance (STANSS): the way a person stands

uniform (YOO-nuh-form): a special set of clothes worn by a team or group

Index

Websites to Visit

www.chiff.com/olympics/olympics-wrestling.htm

www.themat.com

www.wrestlingsbest.com

Further Reading

Chiu, David. *Wrestling: Rules, Tips, Strategy, and Safety*. Rosen Central, 2005.

Crossingham, John. *Wrestling in Action*. Crabtree Publishing Company, 2003.

Ditchfield, Christin. *Wrestling*. Children's Press, 2000.

Murray, Eric. *Wrestling for Fun!* Compass Point Books, 2006.

About the Author

Joanne Mattern is the author of more than 300 books for children. She has written about a variety of subjects, including sports, history, biography, animals, and science. She loves bringing nonfiction subjects to life for children! Joanne lives in New York State with her husband, four children, and assorted pets.

DATE	BORROWER'S NAME
14/05	Amor 2C
3/1/05	Reytha Gia 218
9-11-07	Fran Cuy 208
10-31-07	Robert+9 101
11-13-07	MAV.6
11-13-07	EMMANUEL 215
11-27-07	Jesus Bucio 215
3-2-08	Jose 109
05/20/08	Anigail Saltillo 308
	001529 3246944

DATE	BORROWER'S NAME	
5/4	Axel M.	215
	Jerry	209
9-10	Axel	
	Danielle	115